THE PRINCIPALITY OF SORROWS

by

KEITH BUNIN

Dramatic Publishing
Woodstock, Illinois • London, England • Melbourne, Australia

*** NOTICE ***

DRAMATIC PUBLISHING
P. O. Box 129, Woodstock, Illinois 60098

"Originally presented by Pure Orange Productions, Inc., at Theatre Row Theatre, New York, NY, under the direction of Elizabeth Gottlieb"

Printed in the United States of America

(THE PRINCIPALITY OF SORROWS)

Cover design by Susan Carle

ISBN 0-87129-767-1

IMPORTANT BILLING AND CREDIT REQUIREMENTS

All producers of the Play *must* give credit to the Author(s) of the Play in all programs distributed in connection with performances of the Play and in all instances in which the title of the Play appears for purposes of advertising, publicizing or otherwise exploiting the Play and/or a production. The name of the Author(s) *must* also appear on a separate line, on which no other name appears, immediately following the title, and *must* appear in size of type not less than fifty percent the size of the title type. *On all programs this notice should appear:*

"Produced by special arrangement with
THE DRAMATIC PUBLISHING COMPANY of Woodstock, Illinois"

For Jocelyn Meinhardt

The earth goes on the earth glittering in gold.
The earth goes to the earth sooner than it would.
The earth builds on the earth castles and towers.
The earth says to the earth all this is ours.

Anonymous – 18th century

THE PRINCIPALITY OF SORROWS

A Full-length Play
For 2 Men and 1 Woman, with doubling

CHARACTERS

IRIS/LUCINDA/HOLLY
TEDDY
MARC

PLACE
A garden in a castle in Belgium.

TIME
1923, 1934, and 1947.

THE PRINCIPALITY OF SORROWS was originally produced in New York City by Pure Orange Productions, Inc. (Elizabeth Gottlieb, Sandi Johnson, Elizabeth Timperman, Producers) at the Theatre Row Theatre on December 15, 1995. The production credits were as follows:

CAST (in order of appearance)

Iris/Lucinda/Holly .... JOANNA GOING
Teddy .... ROBERT SEAN LEONARD
Marc .... DAVID LANSBURY

Directed by .... ELIZABETH GOTTLIEB
Set Design by .... HENRY DUNN
Lighting Design by .... JEFF CROITER
Costume Design by .... ANGELINA AVALONE
Sound Design by .... RED RAMONA
Production Stage Manager .. ALEX LYU VOLKHAUSEN
Dramaturg .... JILL RACHEL MORRIS

THE PRINCIPALITY OF SORROWS was workshopped at New York Stage and Film in Poughkeepsie, New York, in June of 1995. I would like to thank everyone who participated in the development of this play, especially Kevin Dewey, Michael Engler, Josh Hamilton, Justin Kirk, Cynthia Nixon, Peter Parnell and Kali Rocha.

ACT ONE

AT RISE: *A summer morning in 1923. The garden is overgrown with flowers, the exotic and the mundane mixed together heedlessly. IRIS is asleep in the gazebo. A small black book, bent back at the spine, rests against her stomach. She is in her late 20s, an impassioned soul hidden behind the pleasant smile of a hostess. TEDDY comes into the garden carrying a bouquet of flowers. He is in his early 20s, wears a well-cut suit and displays a puppy's perpetual hopefulness. IRIS wakes and stands.*

IRIS. Why have you brought me flowers? This is after all a garden.

TEDDY. I thought you'd like them.

IRIS. Clearly you didn't think at all. I'm practically overrun with flowers at the moment. It would've been a far more affectionate gesture for you to bring me a powerful defoliant... who are you?

TEDDY. It's Theodore. *(As IRIS stares blankly.)* Teddy Sterrett.

IRIS *(delighted, clasping his hands in hers)*. Little Teddy Sterrett in long pants now. What are you doing in Belgium of all places? Of course I remember you. Late at night during our parties you'd run down the stairs in your long johns playing off-key on your trumpet.

TEDDY. Yes, well. I was just a boy then.

IRIS. You're still a boy. You won't make me call you Theodore, will you?

TEDDY. You can call me whatever you'd like.

IRIS *(guides TEDDY up to the gazebo)*. Teddy, then. Those parties. I remember my brother Oliver climbing up to the roof of your house in the middle of the worst blizzard.

TEDDY. He caught pneumonia and nearly died.

IRIS. Yes, he was a delicate boy.

TEDDY. And you were always trying to get that awful Marcus Moore to kiss you. I used to sneak out of bed and listen to the two of you in the servants' stairwell, talking for hours about nothing at all.

IRIS. Oh no! It's my worst nightmare that somebody actually heard the treacle that fell off my lips back then. You must've thought me a complete numbskull.

TEDDY. You were the nicest to me by far. I remember New Year's Eve when I was 12. Ollie and Marc and all my sisters were downstairs, but you came up to my bedroom just before midnight and woke me. You said, "I didn't want you to miss the first moment of 1911."

IRIS. My. You have quite a memory, don't you?

TEDDY. Only for certain things.

IRIS. Where have you *been*, Teddy? No, let me guess. Top of your class at—Harvard or Yale, which was it? A little pale from the lack of sun, that's got to be New Haven.

TEDDY. Not quite the top of my class.

IRIS. And now you must be president of one of your father's companies. The button factory or—

TEDDY. The bank.

IRIS. The bank. Well, it could've been anything. Your father does own half the world.

TEDDY. You've been away awhile. He owns two-thirds of the world now.

IRIS. And you're such a sweet boy. When they said the meek shall inherit the earth, little Teddy, I believe they were talking about you specifically. May I offer you a cup of tea?

TEDDY. Please. I caught a cold on the voyage over. You're not terribly secure in this castle. Your maid let me by without a second glance. *(IRIS goes to the service and pours tea for herself and TEDDY.)*

IRIS. All those years of French lessons, *comment allez-vous* and all that, but here they speak some obscure dialect that's barely French at all. Anyway, through some kind of semaphore I helped my maid to understand that I was expecting a guest today, so when you arrived she must have assumed that you were that gentleman.

TEDDY. You're expecting another gentleman?

IRIS. I've been expecting him for an hour already, so whether he is indeed a gentleman is up for debate. But now you've come to see me. I can put away my Shakespeare and enjoy a cup of tea. *(IRIS gives the cup to TEDDY.)*

TEDDY. Oh, what Shakespeare are you reading? He was my favorite in school.

IRIS *(handing him the black book)*. *Titus Andronicus.*

TEDDY. Not one of the Master's finest.

IRIS. Do you think? Actually I prefer it to some of the others. Hamlet and Lear, on the verge of madness and murder but always so well-spoken. Rings a bit false to me. In this one there's no poetry at all, really, just a death or a dismemberment on every page. A lot more true to life, in my opinion. *(IRIS sits back down and sips her tea.)*

TEDDY. I never expressed my condolences for your brother.

IRIS. You were probably still in short pants then.

TEDDY. I was in New Haven. And I didn't find out till I came home for Christmas, and by then it had been months, and I thought you'd probably...put it behind you.

IRIS. There's very little danger of my putting it behind me. But I forgive you for not writing...do you remember my brother at all?

TEDDY. Of course.

IRIS. What do you remember? I'm collecting other people's memories of him to add to my own.

TEDDY. Well. At our parties he came up to my bedroom and drew pictures of me. They were decent pictures, if I remember, but he never got my nose right. Does that help at all?

IRIS. It helps a great deal. Thank you.

TEDDY. He died very bravely, your brother.

IRIS. Well, he died, certainly. I don't know anything about the state of his manhood at the time.

TEDDY. I only meant that—

IRIS. You meant that he died in battle. I just don't like that particular expression.

TEDDY. I'm not sure what you mean.

IRIS *(softening)*. I'm talking nonsense. It was here in Belgium that he died bravely, did you know that? That's part of the reason I came.

TEDDY. Is that why? Your father said that one day you took the last of your savings and set sail without a word to anyone. You've caused a scandal.

IRIS. I never intended that. Traveling is just a good way to find out where it is you want to be when you stop traveling. And my mother *did* spend her last 25 years in this castle. I thought I should at least take a look at it.

TEDDY. It was awfully cruel of her to abandon you and Ollie when you were so young.

IRIS. She was an odd bird. She left me this castle, even though she hadn't seen me since I was a baby, and the rest of her fortune she willed to the care and maintenance of these gardens. Can you imagine? All of that money left to flowers. With her wealth, this place should be pristine till kingdom come. Of course, the way things are headed, kingdom is due to come any day now. But tell me why you've come all the way from New York.

TEDDY. To see you.

IRIS. Don't try to charm me.

TEDDY. But I have. On business. As president of the largest bank on the eastern seaboard, I feel it's my duty to invest some of America's capital in the economies of her war-torn allies. The bank, you see, wants to buy this castle.

IRIS. This castle? You must be joking. There are stones missing at the foundation. The whole place could crumble, literally, as we speak.

TEDDY. The bank has a great deal of business in Belgium, and we feel that the government would look more kindly on our interests if we owned a substantial piece of property here.

IRIS. But why have you chosen this castle of all places?

TEDDY. I learned that you'd inherited it from your mother, and I couldn't imagine that you wanted to live here. I thought you might be willing to sell this place to the bank, and it would be good for everyone.

IRIS. I guess it would, wouldn't it? *(A beat, then, carefully.)* You know, Teddy, I don't believe in the slightest that the president of the Sterrett Bank has nothing better to do than travel all the way here to woo me for my silly castle.

TEDDY. I considered it a priority.

IRIS. Did my father, by chance, have anything to do with this?

TEDDY. I beg your pardon.

IRIS. You said you'd been to see him. Did he in any way influence you to make this trip?

TEDDY. I don't think I can be influenced.

IRIS. He did, didn't he? He's worse than the Germans.

TEDDY. You're being extremely harsh.

IRIS. He bullied my brother to death.

TEDDY. I don't think you can fairly blame your father for—

IRIS. Can't I? My father bullied Oliver into that uniform. He would've bullied him into the grave if he had to.

TEDDY. Your father has always been very nice to—

IRIS. Has he promised to invest in the bank? You should know that he sold all his stock short and it wiped him out. He's poor as a church mouse. And if he was in any way responsible for your coming here, I beg you to confess that to me so you might rid your soul from the clutches of this Antichrist.

TEDDY *(an impetuous confession)*. I wasn't even going to buy the castle for the bank. I was going to pay for it out of my own pocket.

IRIS. Why would you do that?

TEDDY. To help you out of your troubles. Your father said that you don't have any money.

IRIS. My father never asks anyone to take a breath unless it benefits him. So I wonder, what does he want?

TEDDY. The way he represents it, he knows that you hate him but he doesn't understand why.

IRIS. Such a lie.

TEDDY. He sent for me because he said, well, if I'm not betraying a confidence here, he said that you thought you would never marry.

IRIS. I do think that, yes.

TEDDY. And, if I may be so bold, he said that on more than one occasion you had mentioned my name. Favorably, I mean.

IRIS. Now that's just patently ridiculous. You were little Teddy, running down the stairs late at night playing your trumpet. All these years you never entered my mind. *(Slowly TEDDY's face crumples, and he is overcome by sobs.)* Oh no, what's this now? *(Pause.)* Teddy, have you fallen in love with me? *(TEDDY opens his mouth to speak, but the words catch in his throat. He stares at his feet.)* How did this happen? Was I in the room at the time?

TEDDY. It was at our parties. When I was a boy.

IRIS. And my father saw it, and he stored it up in his devil's head just for an occasion like this.

TEDDY *(in sudden, fiery rage)*. Damn him! How dare he lead me on. Does he have any idea who I am?

IRIS. Of course not. In his eyes you're just a large pile of money.

TEDDY. If he *does* have any money left I'll make sure to bankrupt him as soon as I get back to New York.

IRIS. Don't even bother soiling your shoes with him.

TEDDY. Just say the word and I'll crush him between my fingers. It would be a tremendous pleasure.

IRIS. Really, Teddy, that's so sweet of you, but I wouldn't go to any trouble.

TEDDY. He must've mistaken me for a fool.

IRIS *(goes to TEDDY and embraces him)*. You're not a fool at all. You just don't know your own heart yet, and my father saw that, and he took cruel advantage. He did bully you across the ocean, just like he did with Oliver and my mother.

TEDDY *(drawing himself up a little)*. I'll never forgive him for humiliating me in front of you. I apologize for any offense I've caused.

IRIS. I don't blame *you*. And seeing you again is a joy, even in my present misanthropic state.

TEDDY *(with a new, reckless hope)*. Then would you be willing to consider my offer?

IRIS. I can't sell you this castle.

TEDDY. Not that offer.

IRIS. I don't understand.

TEDDY. Would you be willing to consider the offer of my love?

IRIS. Well, that's a far more complicated matter, isn't it?

(MARC comes into the garden, walking with a cane to support his useless left leg. He is in his late 20s, somewhat carelessly dressed, with a downturned smile that

constantly makes you wonder if he is secretly laughing at you.)

MARC. Apologies for my tardiness.

IRIS *(warmly, rising to his assistance)*. Marcus. Do you need help?

MARC. I could negotiate a mountain range. Everybody should have one of these. Your maid thought I was a burglar. It took this cane and all the Walloon French I've mastered to convince her that I was invited. *(TEDDY retreats to the back of the gazebo to compose himself.)*

IRIS. You're more than an hour late. And you were invited four months ago. You can't expect us to be breathlessly awaiting your arrival.

MARC. You don't know how hard it is to disengage yourself from a wife and a child. But you don't appear to be lacking for company.

IRIS *(guides TEDDY over to MARC)*. Don't you recognize this adorable face? This is Teddy Sterrett.

MARC *(recognition lighting his eyes)*. Please. He's Theodore Sterrett now and he's a captain of industry. *(Shaking TEDDY's hand.)* I've read about you in the American papers and I'm suitably impressed.

TEDDY. Iris didn't tell me that you were coming.

IRIS. Teddy and I have been talking about all the parties at his father's house in New York. He told me that he used to listen as you whispered sweet nothings to me in the servants' stairwell.

MARC. I suppose the things I said to you were sweet. They were certainly nothing.

IRIS. That was Teddy's opinion as well. *(Pause.)* So. What are we all doing so far from home? *(TEDDY surrenders himself to sobs. He bolts to leave the garden.)*

TEDDY. I'd better go.

IRIS. Don't be silly.

TEDDY. Really, I'm causing a scene.

IRIS *(going to TEDDY)*. No, don't leave, just take a walk in the garden for a little while.

TEDDY. If I'd known that he was coming—

IRIS. Just take a stroll, enjoy the flowers. *(IRIS dries his tears. TEDDY turns to MARC and speaks with misplaced dignity.)*

TEDDY. It's good to see you again, Marc. Forgive me. I didn't mean to bother anyone. *(TEDDY runs off into the garden. MARC waits until he's out of view, and then starts to laugh, a harsh bark of a laugh that's strangled in his throat.)*

MARC. What a heartbreaker you are.

IRIS. Oh, I didn't break his heart. He broke his own heart. He just used me to do it. He had some help from my father, too.

MARC. How is that awful man? When I was in the service I never felt any remorse about dispatching the Hun's foot soldiers. I just pretended they were all our fathers.

IRIS. My father sent Teddy over here hoping I'd fall in love so he could have a wealthy son-in-law. *(Looking off to where TEDDY has gone.)* Poor Teddy.

MARC. Rich Teddy.

IRIS. Poor Teddy...do you remember all those parties at his father's house? *(MARC sits in the shade on the side of the gazebo, supporting his lame leg on a chair.)*

MARC. I remember the night we went up to the roof and Ollie caught pneumonia.

IRIS. Yes, I remember that most of all.

MARC. We thought he was done for.

IRIS. Luckily he lived to die another day.

MARC. What I remember is the second that he recovered he made it his mission to climb to the top of every tall building in the city.

IRIS. Stupid boy, to tempt fate like that.

MARC. He took us all the way uptown to Grant's tomb. Bribed that park ranger to let us onto the roof in the middle of the night. *(IRIS goes to the tea service, refills her cup and pours a new cup for MARC.)*

IRIS. It *was* beautiful, though, wasn't it? We could see all the way down to the Battery.

MARC. A tomb with a view, that was his joke. We finally had a tomb with a view.

IRIS. I can't tell if we were all stupid or splendid then. Throwing ourselves into the night with such abandon that just living through it could be considered a triumph. And you, making love to me in the servants' stairwell till the wee hours of the morning.

MARC. I was very conceited.

IRIS. Yes, but you were so bent on involving me in all your conceits, that your self-absorption became something resembling generosity. I don't think you loved me then.

MARC. I was in love with the sound of my own voice. That's about all.

IRIS. The last time I saw you was more than seven years ago. Can you believe that? The day you and Oliver shipped out to fight with the British Army. My father had all the newspapers there. I bought a new dress. I thought it was the most wonderful thing in the world.

MARC. I guess this is the point where I'm supposed to tell you that you haven't aged a day.

IRIS. Please. We've both aged horribly.

MARC. Well, I'm a cripple. I'm supposed to look horrible. It's part of my special charm.

IRIS. I *am* sorry.

MARC. It's nothing.

IRIS. Always the stiff upper lip.

MARC. I'm not being valiant, just literal. My leg has been deprived of all use and feeling. It's unnecessary, superfluous: in a word, nothing. It's hardly worth grieving for.

IRIS. But still.

MARC *(with a genuine surge of feeling)*. Thank you for your concern. *(They are a little too close to each other now. IRIS hands the cup of tea to MARC.)* Would you have any objection if I add my own sweetener to the tea?

IRIS. Certainly not. In fact, I'll demand some for myself. *(MARC takes a flask from his pocket and pours liberal doses of whiskey into the cups of tea.)* I don't believe you've told me your wife's name.

MARC. Leontine.

IRIS. That's very pretty. And she's well?

MARC *(shaking his head)*. My stipend from the army barely pays for my cigarettes, so she's gone to work in a millinery. She's there six days a week from dawn till dusk, soaking pieces of felt in some kind of acid that's eating her hands away. She barely even has fingernails anymore.

IRIS. She must love you very much, to break her back like that.

MARC. She'd have to do it anyway. It's work. Everyone in the world does it besides you and me.

IRIS. I'd like to meet her sometime.

MARC. Maybe once she's learned some more English.

IRIS. I'd never have predicted this kind of marriage for you.

MARC *(smiling grimly)*. Well, there is Marcus Jr. to consider. *(MARC downs his spiked tea in one gulp. IRIS rises to take MARC's empty cup from him, and wobbles a little on her feet.)* Are you all right?

IRIS. It's just the whiskey on an empty stomach.

MARC. Should I send for the maid to get you some bread?

IRIS. There isn't any in the house. I spent the last of my savings on the voyage, I don't have a lot left over for food.

MARC. What do you mean? Your father's rich as Croesus.

IRIS. He galloped us into bankruptcy long ago.

MARC. I had no idea.

IRIS. And you'd think my mother would've planted at least one apple tree, but no luck.

MARC. But you can't starve yourself.

IRIS. It's all better now... did you ever expect to see me in a garden? I'm such a city girl.

MARC. You *are* named Iris.

IRIS. My mother loved flowers.

MARC. Apparently.

IRIS. She left her entire fortune to this place. Not a nickel to family or friends or charities. It's all in a trust and every month the gardener receives a check for labor and services.

MARC. That's a novel way to waste a fortune.

IRIS. You shouldn't speak ill of my mother's gardens. Apparently her ashes are scattered just beneath our feet.

MARC. It's a beautiful place. This gazebo is a bit odd, though.

IRIS. Isn't it? A little touch of Newport in the Ardennes. I guess my dear old mama couldn't escape her home country entirely.

MARC. When we were growing up you said she ran away because she fell in love with the prince of Belgium. I never quite believed you.

IRIS. Yes, I made that up. I thought it sounded romantic. The truth is I don't know why she left. When I came here I searched the entire estate hoping to find a diary, or a letter, anything that might have explained... but there's nothing. There *is* a portrait of her up in the bedroom. It gave me a shock: Papa banished all traces of her from the house, so it was the first time I ever saw her face.

MARC. And what did she look like?

IRIS. Like me. She looked exactly like me. *(Pause.)* She must've loved all this. She wouldn't leave even when everything around her was a battlefield.

MARC. When I was in the service here the land was so pockmarked with shellholes that we couldn't walk in a straight line, and we could never figure out where we were because all the landmarks on our maps had been destroyed.

IRIS. What was Oliver like in the army?

MARC. I've made a concerted effort to draw a veil over those years.

IRIS. And you wouldn't disturb it, even for me?

MARC. Not for all the rice in China. I hope this isn't why you invited me. I'd hate to disappoint such a pretty girl.

IRIS. There's no need to disappoint me. Just lift the veil a little. *(MARC removes two cigarettes from his gold cigarette box.)*

MARC. He was the worst soldier in the whole company. Too much of a rich boy, too used to having the run of the place. He would make fun of the accents of the Brits who commanded us. Me, I knew they were stupid men, but at least they were smarter than I was about how to keep us alive. Ollie was good at drawing pictures and getting drunk, and there wasn't much call for those talents at war. *(MARC lights the cigarettes and hands one to IRIS.)*

IRIS. And the day he died?

MARC. You're full of questions today, aren't you?

IRIS. I'd like to understand.

MARC. I wouldn't go rooting around in *my* memory for understanding. Trust me, there's no profit in it.

IRIS. I went to the battlefield where he fell. The first day I got here.

MARC. What on earth did you expect to find there?

IRIS. It was the last place that he was alive. I wanted to see if there was even a trace of him left. And there isn't. But you were with him, and you can tell me what happened. Please?

MARC *(after a long moment of consideration)*. I was talking to Ollie over coffee one morning when a shell burst beside us. It was so close that we found ourselves at the bottom of the crater it had made. I crawled up the side of the crater and turned to give my arm to Ollie. But his arm had been severed from his body and was just held in place by a bit of his sleeve. Then another shell burst at his feet and it was over.

IRIS *(takes a deep drag off her cigarette)*. I had to identify his body once it was shipped back to the States, because Papa was in his cups. It wasn't really his body anymore, it was ... how did they say? His remains. But nothing really remained. I sat in the army morgue, cursing my father, cursing America, cursing myself ... I don't know how long it was till I stopped.

MARC. I don't think you've stopped yet. It was a terrible war. We'll never see its equal.

IRIS. If I were a gambler, I'd wager you the entire world that you're wrong about that. And you would have to pay.

(TEDDY wanders through the garden behind them, pacing back and forth, swinging a tree branch wildly.)

MARC. Your lover is decapitating the roses.

IRIS. It's so strange to talk with Teddy. He's only five or six years younger than we are, but he missed the war entirely. And he acts like everything's been set out just for him.

MARC. Everything but you.

IRIS. I couldn't make him happy.

MARC. That doesn't matter. You're his first love. Those last forever. He'll hang your portrait on the inside of his eye for the rest of his life.

IRIS. That's very melodramatic.

MARC. On the contrary, it's pitifully common.

IRIS. How do you know so much about this? I thought you were only in love with the sound of your own voice.

MARC. During the war I dreamt of you on occasion.

IRIS. Don't say pretty things to me.

MARC. I've kept this for quite some time. *(MARC removes a photograph from his pocket and hands it to IRIS.)*

IRIS. This was Oliver's.

MARC. I was permitted to keep something of his. This is what I chose.

IRIS. You kept my photograph when you were at war? You didn't even write.

MARC. It was better just to have a photograph.

IRIS. And you still carry it with you?

MARC. I brought it today because I thought you might like to have it.

(TEDDY wanders back into view and conceals himself clumsily behind a large bush.)

IRIS. I would, thank you. I'll hang it on the inside of my eye, to remind me that two men went away to war meaning to come back to me, but in the end neither one of them did. *(Suddenly shifting her gaze to MARC.)* May I ask you something? Do you love your wife?

MARC. I thought she was very pretty for a few minutes several years ago.

IRIS. So you feel nothing for her?

MARC. I don't believe that question has ever occurred to me.

IRIS. I'm sorry.

MARC. If I get lonely there's always a remedy, for just a small fee.

IRIS. Now why did you tell me that? If I met your wife tomorrow, I'd find it very difficult to talk to her because I'd already be keeping a terrible secret.

MARC. If you met my wife tomorrow you'd find it very difficult to talk to her because she barely speaks English. And you don't want to meet my wife.

IRIS. Why not?

MARC. Because you want to kiss me.

IRIS. Is that what you think?

MARC. Why else would you have invited me here?

IRIS. Maybe I just wanted to talk with an old friend.

MARC *(advancing on her)*. We were never friends.

IRIS. What were we, then?

MARC. I was an obnoxious little dandy. And you were a spoiled girl.

IRIS. It's lucky we're grown up now.

MARC. Yes, and your beauty's faded, and I'm a cripple, so there's really no point in being coy. Let's just do now what we didn't do then, out of honor and chastity and sentiment.

IRIS. Well. When you put it as sweetly as that. *(MARC kisses IRIS on the mouth. She struggles for a moment, and then gives in and even responds. TEDDY watches as the kiss gets more fervid and impassioned, until IRIS finally pulls herself away.)* I didn't ask you to come so I could kiss you. That would be far too desperate to be of any use. But you and Oliver are the only two people in the world I've ever loved. And in the same way that I had to see the place where he died, I had to know if what I loved about you was lost in the war. And the good part of you *has* snapped and broken, just like it has in me. *(In quiet triumph.)* And now I'm not bound to anything on earth. *(Pause.)* Do you want your photograph back?

MARC. I won't be needing it. *(IRIS rips up the photograph and lets the pieces fall to the ground.)* You should know, there's no reason to get so sentimental over Ollie. He wasn't much of a man. I doubt he'd have amounted to anything even if he did survive the war.

IRIS. Like us, then. We survived the war and we haven't amounted to anything. No, all the things I loved—you, Oliver, my dresses, the parties at Teddy's house—they're all dead and gone, and on reflection they weren't worth very much to begin with. And for the life of me I can't decide which is worse.

MARC. I don't think that we'll ever see each other again.

IRIS. No, we won't. But isn't it nice to know all these things for sure? *(MARC holds IRIS's gaze for a moment, and then turns and shakes his cane into the bushes.)*

MARC. She's all yours. I hope you have better luck with her. *(MARC smiles at IRIS and walks out of the garden. IRIS sits back down.)*

IRIS. You can come out of there now.

(TEDDY stumbles out of the bushes, his clothes and hair dirty and covered with sticks and leaves. IRIS does not look at him.)

TEDDY. I'm sorry.

IRIS. How much did you hear?

TEDDY. More than I wanted to.

IRIS. I couldn't make you happy.

TEDDY. You're wrong about that. Marry me and every door in the world will open for you. We'll fight your father and everything else you hate. We'll build schools and museums and name them all after Oliver. And we'll plant a garden in the back of our house where all our children can play.

IRIS. Little Teddy. How I pity you.

TEDDY. Pity me? Why? *(IRIS looks at TEDDY. She takes in his disheveled condition, and starts to laugh despite herself.)* What's so funny?

IRIS. You look like you've been on safari!

TEDDY. Do I? *(TEDDY looks down at himself. His sense of humor is awakened, and he laughs along with IRIS. IRIS rises and goes to TEDDY.)*

IRIS. Let me help you. You've got all these things stuck in your hair... *(IRIS and TEDDY are consumed with laughter. TEDDY suddenly clutches her arm tightly.)*

TEDDY. Can you blame me for being in love with you? *(IRIS stares at TEDDY. She stops laughing, and the color drains from her face. She looks drawn and haggard and suddenly much older.)*

IRIS. Oh, it's just an echo. Trust me: there's nothing good here anymore. *(Picking the last few burrs from his hair.)* There you are. Like new. *(IRIS embraces TEDDY. She unclasps from him. TEDDY persists in holding his arms out to her, then gives up and shoves his hands uselessly into his pockets.)* I'd like you to do me a favor. Tomorrow you'll set sail for New York and when you return I want you to visit my father. Tell him that if he sends any more suitors, I'll turn them away at the door.

TEDDY. I'll send you money.

IRIS. I'll send it back... it's been quite a morning.

TEDDY. Would you mind if I sit with you for a while?

IRIS. Of course I wouldn't mind. *(TEDDY sits next to IRIS. He picks up the black book from the table.)*

TEDDY. How does this play end? I never finished it.

IRIS. How do they all end? Everyone dies, and there's a new emperor, and everything starts all over again.

TEDDY. I guess that's what tragedy is.

IRIS *(a little chidingly)*. That's what *history* is. *(Pause.)* I think I'll let you have this garden after all. But if you don't mind I'll give it to you free of charge. I'll leave it to you in my will. That way maybe you'll come back here. It'll be nice to know somebody's looking at it.

TEDDY. If that's what you want.

IRIS. It is. *(Pause.)* The sun's putting me to sleep. *(IRIS closes her eyes. TEDDY watches her for a long moment.)*

TEDDY. Iris? *(IRIS sleeps. He carefully gathers up the tiny pieces of her photograph from the ground and collects them in his lap.)*

END OF ACT ONE

ACT TWO

AT RISE: *A summer afternoon in 1934. Rain taps lightly on the roof of the gazebo. The sky is grey. MARC, in his late 30s, dressed in dirty overalls, works in the garden. In one hand he holds his cane; in the other he awkwardly wields a large pair of shears. MARC's lifelong cynicism is under attack from a newly-acquired middle-aged sentimentality. TEDDY, in his early 30s, dressed in a well-tailored but deeply worn suit, runs into the garden from the castle. In one hand he holds the umbrella that is opened over his head; in the other he clutches a ledger stuffed thick with papers. TEDDY displays the quixotic determination of the utterly defeated.*

TEDDY. Why did it have to rain today?

MARC. Because God hates you.

TEDDY. Is that Marcus Moore? Your son just let us into the castle. He's the spitting image of you. And so tall! *(MARC emerges from the bushes and extends a muddied hand to TEDDY.)*

MARC. And he's only 14. I've built a Colossus. Little Teddy Sterrett. That's quite a suit you're wearing.

TEDDY. It's supposed to make me look imposing.

MARC. It doesn't work.

TEDDY. That's obvious. Did you get my wire?

MARC. Of course. Did you bring your wife? *(TEDDY gets under cover inside the gazebo and closes his umbrella.)*

TEDDY. She's trying to charm the baron up in the castle. I promised myself I'd look over the briefs in private before I sign even a blade of grass over to him. *(Opening his ledger.)* He's not even a real baron. He bought his title, along with everything else in Belgium, after he made his fortune speculating in these mines.

MARC. I know the baron. Five years ago he found coal just over that hill. Since then he's dug up all the land from here to town.

TEDDY. Yes, when I came here to see Iris, there was only countryside for miles around.

MARC. And it seems pretty silly to tend a garden in the middle of all these mines. *(Pause.)* Are you really going to sell the estate to that bastard?

TEDDY. I'm going to try and hold on to Iris's garden. It's just this small patch of land from the castle to the pond. I don't see why he wouldn't be able to just dig around it...I'm sorry. It's so strange to see you here.

MARC. It's been 11 years.

TEDDY. Not the years.

MARC. I don't think Iris could possibly have been serious when she appointed me gardener in her will. She probably just wanted to poke a little fun at me from beyond the grave. But it's been a good job. And my son Marcus needs to be in the country for his health: he has an irregular heartbeat.

TEDDY. Well. At least you get to live in a castle.

MARC. I wouldn't be caught dead in that drafty old barn. Do you see that shack? I built it myself, when Leontine was nursing Marcus Jr. through pneumonia. You should've seen me out in the dirt, hopping around on one leg. I brought off some pretty astounding maneuvers.

TEDDY. Look at it. Those diamond-shaped windows: it's my father's country estate done over as a doll house.

MARC. Is it? I never noticed that before. Leontine's in there now.

TEDDY. When I go up to the house I'll tell Lucinda to say hello.

MARC. She's embarrassed to be around Americans. Her English is weak.

TEDDY. By the way, for my wife's peace of mind I told her that this castle was left to me by my maiden aunt. Obviously nothing happened between Iris and me, and it was long before my marriage anyway, but Lucinda's insanely jealous. I'd appreciate if you don't contradict the story I've told her.

MARC. Your wife must be incredibly devoted to you.

TEDDY. She's a wonderful woman. *(Pause.)* Did you ever see Iris, after ... the last time we all saw each other?

MARC *(shaking his head)*. I did go to the funeral. She asked to be burnt, and for her ashes to be scattered here. That was my first duty as gardener.

TEDDY. Do you ever think about her?

MARC. Quite often.

TEDDY. It was a good thing, loving her. Even when I was too young to warrant a second glance. Even when she was an ocean away. The truth is I didn't need to be in her arms or even in her thoughts. I just needed her to be alive in the world. Knowing that she was ... gave *shape* to things.

MARC. Eleven years ago you loved her and she couldn't love you back, and she loved me and I couldn't love her back. No grand passions, just a couple of collisions. Let's just put it all behind us, shall we? *(Taking out his gold box of cigarettes.)* Would you like one? They're really wonderful. Ypres cigarettes. Only made here in Belgium. These are the reason I left America. *(MARC takes two cigarettes from the box, lights them, and hands one to TEDDY.)*

TEDDY. Honestly?

MARC. I should let you in on a new thing called sarcasm.

TEDDY. Well, you could've left America because of the cigarettes, for all I know. *(TEDDY takes a drag off the cigarette and coughs wildly.)*

MARC. They're ludicrously strong, I know.

TEDDY. I hope you didn't leave America for *this.*

MARC. I never even try to explain to Americans why I left America. *(Pause.)* If the baron won't accept your terms, what will you do?

TEDDY. I'll probably have to sell him the entire estate.

MARC. And then what will happen to me?

TEDDY. Well.

MARC. It's a foolish, weak question, I know, but there we are: what will happen to me?

TEDDY. It isn't that simple. I'm sure you can understand.

MARC. Goddamn you to hell, then.

TEDDY. Not that I need to explain myself to you—

MARC. Oh no, God forbid.

TEDDY. —but selling this place would be very good for me—

MARC. If you start talking about margins of profit, I'll beat you to death with my cane.

TEDDY. —and who knows if anyone's going to make an offer like this again.

MARC. Spare me the sob story. We both know that this is all about how you need to put the down payment on a yacht you want to buy from the Sheik of Araby.

TEDDY. Nothing could be further from the—

MARC. And your daddy can't front you because all his cash is tied up in interest-free municipal bonds.

TEDDY. It's staggering how little you understand.

MARC. You'll be killing my son, I hope you know that.

TEDDY. Today I can't be thinking about you.

MARC. What an American you are. I might as well be speaking Walloon French myself.

(LUCINDA, in her late 20s, comes into the garden from the house, holding one palm over her head to shield herself from the rain. LUCINDA possesses a gentle, undiscerning empathy that is the result of never having been loved in her life. MARC rises with a start: either he knows her or, more likely, he knows a woman who looks almost exactly like her.)

LUCINDA. I'm sorry to interrupt, Theodore, but I can't stall the baron any longer.

TEDDY. Is he getting impatient?

LUCINDA. Worse. He's getting patient. The cat who swallowed the canary. It's just, the longer you stay out here, the more he'll think that he's got you painted into a corner.

TEDDY. I'm just softening him up for the kill, my love. Lucinda, I'd like you to meet Marcus Moore. Marc, this is my wife. *(MARC goes to LUCINDA and kisses her hand, giving her a deep courtly bow in his muddy overalls.)*

MARC. I'm very pleased.

LUCINDA. You're an American.

TEDDY. Don't get him started on that. I have some business to do.

LUCINDA. I'm sure you'll slay him, my love.

TEDDY. I appreciate your faith. Well. Once more into the breach. *(TEDDY steadies his gait as he walks up to the house. LUCINDA stares after him. MARC has not taken his eyes from LUCINDA. She notices this, and her hand goes to her mouth. She lets out a small cry of despair.)*

MARC. Forgive me, but I—It's just—

LUCINDA. You're going to say I look like someone.

MARC. Almost exactly, yes.

LUCINDA. One of the reasons I came to Belgium, I thought, at least over here we won't run into anyone who knew her. But I'm out of luck again, I see. *(Pause.)* I'm sorry, but... Theodore told me that this castle was left to him by his maiden aunt. I don't think that's true anymore. *(As MARC looks down at his feet.)* Would I also be right if I guessed that this castle was really owned by Iris Bell? *(MARC continues staring at the ground.)* Please?

MARC. I'd rather not talk about Iris.

LUCINDA. Theodore won't ever talk about her. Not a word. Finally I found a photograph in the bottom of his chest of drawers. Someone had ripped it up but he had pieced it back together like it was a jigsaw puzzle. Even with the glue covering part of her face I could tell that she looked exactly like me. *(A quiet plea.)* Could she really have been all that extraordinary?

MARC. It was a long time ago.

LUCINDA. You knew her in New York, then? From the way you kissed my hand I know you haven't always been a gardener.

MARC. When we were children, Iris and I went to parties at Teddy's house.

LUCINDA. Nobody calls him Teddy. He'd throw a fit if they did. *(Pause.)* May I ask, how did she die? Everyone in New York says something completely different.

MARC. I'd say suicide, but that's a far more melodramatic course of action than she'd ever take. She simply let nothing stand between herself and death. Once she set her mind to anything, she was steadfast. I always admired that.

LUCINDA. The reason she killed herself—it didn't have anything to do with Theodore, did it?

MARC *(shaking his head)*. It was amazing, what happened to her. When we were children she used to run down Fifth Avenue, tossing bags of cookies into any open windows. I'd long since given up on America, but when Iris died, that's when I knew it was over. If the joy could go out of her ... where did you come from?

LUCINDA. What do you mean?

MARC. Teddy couldn't very well place an advertisement in the Tribune.

LUCINDA. Have you ever heard of a town called Shamokin? It's in Pennsylvania.

MARC. I've heard of Pennsylvania.

LUCINDA. Well, Shamokin is a town in Pennsylvania that exists entirely to make every other place in the world look wonderful by comparison. Just after I turned 18 I ran away to New York. I got a job as a stenographer.

MARC. An exciting and lucrative profession.

LUCINDA. One morning I was eating breakfast in the Empire Coffee Shop when Theodore tapped me on the shoulder. "Excuse me," he said, "but you're the most beautiful girl I've ever seen."

MARC. A millionaire taps a stenographer on the shoulder and tells her she's beautiful.

LUCINDA. I thought I was living in a picture show. He proposed on our second date. *(LUCINDA holds out her hand to MARC. He stares at the large ring on her finger.)*

MARC. Are all those diamonds?

LUCINDA. So I'm told. They feel like millstones. It's funny, isn't it, to realize what a lie it's all been.

MARC. After a shell took my leg, I spent months in the hospital and every day the chaplain would come and tell me it was God's will. I would have killed myself then, but I didn't want to give God the satisfaction of sending me to hell. Then I realized the chaplain was lying to me: God didn't will any of this to happen. God's just standing around watching everything, at least as horrified as I am and just as powerless to stop it. And then I started to think of all the other lies I'd been told. My father telling me that I had an obligation to my country. My sergeant telling me that the Germans were no better than pigs. That particular American type of lie, dripping with duty and honor and misplaced pride.

LUCINDA. That I think I understand.

MARC. I've lived a solitary life taking care of this garden for 11 years, and God has sent down hurricanes, hailstorms, and blizzards. But I'd take the worst monsoon over the prospect of having another American look me in the face and tell me a lie.

LUCINDA. Well, I'm glad all you did is leave. I'm glad you didn't kill yourself, is what I mean. *(MARC considers LUCINDA very closely. Suddenly he shifts his gaze from her, looking deeper into the garden.)*

MARC. Oh, there he is. That's my son. By the acacia tree.

LUCINDA. He's so tall. He's already a grown man.

MARC. He has quite a knack for gardening, which is something I certainly can't say for myself. He works out here all day and stays up reading botany all night. He breathes this place. He knows the English, French, and Latin for every flower, and he knows what they all mean.

LUCINDA. What they mean?

MARC. Yes, if you give someone a yellow tulip it means one thing, but a red tulip means something else entirely. The language of flowers, it's called, and my boy speaks it fluently. If the garden ever dries up I'll show you some of his handiwork. Anyway, when I look at him I don't feel like depriving the world of my illustrious presence.

LUCINDA. Theodore and I have a son.

MARC. He didn't mention that.

LUCINDA. I'm not surprised. Theodore Jr.—Teddy, we call him—he's very sensitive. A little nervous even—he's always having nightmares. Theodore doesn't like him. But he's my pride and joy. You know, every night before I go to bed, I pray that Teddy will grow up healthy and strong. But the truth is I'm not sure I'm praying *for* him; I think I'm really praying *to* him. Somehow I feel if he could just be happy, it would make up for so many other things. Do you ever feel that way about your boy?

MARC. All the time.

LUCINDA *(peering up toward the house)*. I wonder what's going on in there.

MARC. Why are the two of you so nervous about the baron? This estate can't be worth one percent of the Sterrett fortune.

LUCINDA. I'm afraid this estate is 100 percent of the Sterrett fortune.

MARC. I don't understand.

LUCINDA. We don't have any money, Theodore and I.

MARC. I know times are tough now, but I can't believe—

LUCINDA. Theodore's father is still very rich. But Theodore's been disinherited.

MARC. Why?

LUCINDA. Because of me.

MARC. How do you mean?

LUCINDA. Theodore's father thought I was the wrong wife for him.

MARC. And I thought he was going to sell this place just out of spite.

LUCINDA. That's Theodore. He'd rather you think him a tyrant than a pauper.

MARC. I'm afraid he's both.

LUCINDA. Every night I stretch half a can of beans into a full dinner and then Teddy and I clear the table and watch Theodore do the books. Accounting for all our debts, tallying up all our losses. And I add it all together for myself, too. What poor investments we've made, Theodore and I. And all that time I thought we were in this together. *(Without realizing it, LUCINDA has started to cry. MARC removes his handkerchief and starts to dry her tears.)*

MARC. Here. Let me.

LUCINDA. No, I'm sick of trying to stop them. Theodore says once we're rich again he's going to bankrupt his father. He doesn't care about us, he's all bitterness and spite.

MARC *(puts his arm around LUCINDA and holds her consolingly)*. I'm so sorry.

LUCINDA. Oh, things aren't all bad. It's stopped raining, for one.

(Despite herself, LUCINDA starts to giggle. MARC draws her a little closer to him, and they sit, hopeless but laughing, in the rain. TEDDY comes back down from the house and considers them.)

TEDDY. You two seem to be enjoying yourselves, in any event. I'm glad to see Marc can still charm the ladies.

LUCINDA *(drying her eyes)*. Oh, Theodore, for heaven's sake ... what did the baron say?

TEDDY. He won't buy the estate without the garden.

LUCINDA. And—you'll accept?

TEDDY. I don't know. *(LUCINDA opens her mouth to speak to TEDDY, but then thinks better of it and turns to MARC.)*

LUCINDA. Mr. Moore—

MARC. Marc.

LUCINDA. Marc ... would you mind leaving us alone for a few minutes?

MARC *(nods, rising)*. If you'd like to take a stroll in the garden while you talk, feel free. *(MARC leaves the gazebo and disappears deeper into the garden. TEDDY stands unprotected in the rain.)*

TEDDY. The baron didn't even have to say a word. He just let me talk myself into a corner.

LUCINDA. You were in a corner to begin with. The baron was never going to buy the estate without the garden. Now you just have to negotiate the best price possible. You can certainly do that. You're a wonderful businessman.

TEDDY. My father is a wonderful businessman, I'm a serviceable apprentice.

LUCINDA. He was just born at a better time—

TEDDY. And damn him, for making me so much softer than he is.

LUCINDA. Why do you always blame your father whenever something isn't going your way? It can't possibly help matters.

TEDDY. It's directly his fault that we're in this mess.

LUCINDA. Your maiden aunt loved you very much, I guess.

TEDDY. And she loved her gardens even more. She wanted them kept up.

LUCINDA. You never talk about her.

TEDDY. I was just a boy.

LUCINDA. I'm not being fair. I should tell you I know you're lying.

TEDDY. What did Marc say to you?

LUCINDA. You should've warned him that I look exactly like her. I guess he was very attached to her, too.

TEDDY. With Marc it was a case of too little too late.

(MARC sneaks back into view. He watches TEDDY and LUCINDA from the garden, taking occasional swigs from his whiskey flask.)

LUCINDA. Well, she seems to still have quite a hold on both of you. *(Pause.)* Please tell me: did you have an affair with her?

TEDDY. Get your mind out of the gutter.

LUCINDA. I'm trying to understand, Theodore—

TEDDY. It's a disgusting conversation and I don't want any part of it.

LUCINDA. You fell in love with a woman who died: isn't that what happened? If you tell me about it I might be able to help.

TEDDY. I didn't have an affair with her. I came to see her once. I asked her to marry me, and she said no.

LUCINDA. Because of Marc?

TEDDY. Because she wanted to die.

LUCINDA. That's tragic.

TEDDY. That's how I felt at the time.

LUCINDA. But you can't make her tragedy your own.

TEDDY. I don't see how you could understand.

LUCINDA. I understand very well that you live inside this bubble of could-bes and never-weres. You've built a kingdom for yourself in the past, where Iris Bell falls in love with you and you save her life. And you've built a kingdom for yourself in the future, where you get so rich you can buy all of New York and bankrupt your father in the bargain. But the past and future aren't real. There's only today and then today again. And if you aren't building your kingdom with what you have today... well, then, it's just castles in the air, my love. *(MARC stealthily disappears further into the garden.)*

TEDDY. So what are you telling me? Do you want to leave?

LUCINDA. No.

TEDDY. Why on earth would you stay?

LUCINDA. Because we have a son. Ten years ago you threw everything over because of her, and you destroyed the both of us. That doesn't matter, but if you do it again you'll destroy Teddy, and that I can't bear.

TEDDY. No one is going to be destroyed.

LUCINDA. I may look like Iris Bell, but Teddy looks like you. And if you don't see yourself when you look at him, then you're no longer human. Does the boy mean anything to you, Theodore? That's all I need to know.

TEDDY *(smiling grimly)*. My goodness. What have I done to you?

LUCINDA. Oh, my love. You need to get out of debt and start again. You have to sell this castle... *(Taking off her ring.)* ... or you can sell this. If you sell the ring, I'll take Teddy back with me to Shamokin and you'll never have to see us again. If you sell the castle, you can forget about this woman who never loved you anyway and we can make another try at it.

TEDDY. Between you and the baron, I've received more than my fair share of ultimatums today. *(LUCINDA takes the ring, puts it in TEDDY's palm, and closes his hand around it.)*

LUCINDA. I wonder what you're going to do.

TEDDY. You're not the only one.

(TEDDY walks off toward the house. LUCINDA watches after him. MARC emerges from the garden, holding two flowers and a tree branch in his free hand.)

MARC. It's too muddy to take you into the garden, so I brought you some cuttings.

LUCINDA. That's very nice of you. *(Taking the branch from him.)* What's this?

MARC. It's from an acacia tree. In the language of flowers, according to my son, the acacia is the flower of the graveyard. It all means something. And every flower means something different upside-down, or on a different part of your body. *(Handing her a large marigold.)* A marigold worn on the head, for example, is a sorrow of the mind, and a marigold on the heart is a sorrow of love.

LUCINDA *(lightly)*. I should be covered from head to toe with marigolds. The language of flowers. Who made it up?

MARC. Probably a man who was too ashamed to say what he really meant. He was in love with a girl, so he picked a flower, gave it to her, and hoped she would understand without him having to say anything. *(MARC hands the last of his flowers to LUCINDA.)*

LUCINDA. This smells like oranges.

MARC. It's a Little Darling. A mingonette, if you want to know the real name.

LUCINDA. And what does it mean, do you know?

MARC. It's the flower of healing love. *(Taking her hand carefully.)* What's happened to your ring?

LUCINDA. I've just forced Theodore to choose between me and your late friend. What's awful is I don't think I'm going to win.

MARC. If he sells the castle then I lose my home.

LUCINDA. If he sells the ring then I lose *my* home.

MARC. Then I guess we're enemies.

LUCINDA. I hope not. If we are, we're enemies only by circumstance.

MARC. Enemies all the same. I had nothing against the Germans, but I killed a lot of them anyway. *(Very lightly.)* It's too bad, really. I was going to suggest that the two of us run away together.

LUCINDA *(laughing, delighted)*. Where would we go?

MARC. Wherever the wind carries us.

LUCINDA. What about your wife?

MARC. She won't notice that I'm gone.

LUCINDA. What about my husband?

MARC. Do I really have to dignify that with an answer?

LUCINDA *(bristling a little, but taking it lightly)*. Now you're being cruel. And our sons?

MARC. We'll take them with us. We'll baptize them into the vagabond life.

LUCINDA. And what will we do for money?

MARC. Money will be no object for us, because we won't be ruled by it like Teddy is. We'll just travel, making ourselves useful and merry, and money will come.

LUCINDA. You're a lot more naive than I first thought you were.

MARC. It's my theory that if a man and a woman are together, doing what they want most of all, then the world can't help but make allowances.

LUCINDA. What about your theory of a solitary life?

MARC. Well, theories are never absolute. They're provisional, good only until a better theory comes along.

LUCINDA. And I'm that better theory?

MARC. I certainly hope so. *(MARC's eyes are locked onto LUCINDA. LUCINDA looks away.)*

LUCINDA. You're serious, aren't you?

MARC. Did you think I was joking?

LUCINDA. I don't know what I thought.

MARC. You're a very special woman.

LUCINDA. You've known me for an hour. I'm sorry...I should never have let you take things so far. I can't go with you.

MARC. You'd be making a big mistake not to.

LUCINDA. You said that if a man and a woman are doing what they want most of all...well, traveling with you isn't what I want most of all.

MARC. Well, what *do* you want most of all? Maybe I could accommodate you.

LUCINDA. I only think about what I *need* these days. I can't remember the last time I considered what I *want.* *(Considers seriously for a moment.)* I guess what I want is that when Theodore tapped me on the shoulder in the Empire Coffee Shop, and said that I was the most beautiful girl he'd ever seen...I want him to have really meant what he said. Because then I wouldn't have wasted the last 10 years. And my boy would have a father. That's what I want most of all. And traveling with you couldn't change that. Besides, even with you I'd always look like someone else. *(Pause.)* This woman—Iris—you were in love with her, too?

MARC. No. But I think that if I could've been, at the right moment, I would've saved her life.

LUCINDA. That's not your fault.

MARC. Yes it is. I'm afraid you don't know me very well. *(Suddenly rising.)* Would you be terribly offended if I asked to kiss you?

LUCINDA *(nervously)*. I don't think that would be a good idea...

MARC *(aggressively advancing on her).* Please let me. I've given up on the rest of our lives. I'd be happy with a good 10 seconds. Please?

LUCINDA. No, I—

(LUCINDA moves to get away, but MARC is too fast for her, and pins her down with a kiss. TEDDY comes back down from the house clutching his ledger. He freezes. LUCINDA wrenches herself away from MARC, knocking his cane away from him in the process. MARC instinctively starts after LUCINDA but loses his balance and falls to the ground helplessly.)

TEDDY. Well.

LUCINDA *(mortified).* Oh, for heaven's sake.

MARC. Don't blame your wife, I was just trying to get her to pity me.

TEDDY. That's the oldest trick in the book. And in your case one of the easiest.

MARC. I see you're trying out that newfangled sarcasm. *(TEDDY reaches out his hand to help MARC up. MARC slaps TEDDY's hand away. TEDDY decides to ignore MARC, and turns to LUCINDA.)*

TEDDY. The baron asked me to send you his regards.

LUCINDA. He's left already?

TEDDY. He's a busy man. And I kept him waiting long enough. But I've kept you waiting a lot longer, haven't I?

LUCINDA. I suppose. *(TEDDY takes out the ring and holds it carefully in his hand.)*

TEDDY. You said this doesn't belong to you. And as I was walking up to the castle I could feel it in my pocket, weighing me down, and I realized that it doesn't belong to *me*, either. It occurred to me that I should give it to someone. I decided it should be the woman who'd stay with me even after I'd lost our home. The woman who'd travel all the way here to entertain a truly loathsome baron just so I could get out of debt. And, not incidentally, the woman who is the mother of my son. And then it occurred to me that this does belong to you after all. *(Holding the ring out to LUCINDA.)* What do you think, my love? *(LUCINDA slowly moves to TEDDY and takes the ring from him. They embrace cautiously. MARC stares at the ground.)*

LUCINDA. Please, can we leave right away?

TEDDY. Tell the driver we're ready. I'll be with you directly. *(LUCINDA starts up toward the house. Suddenly she stops, aware that she ought to say something to MARC, at least out of politeness.)*

LUCINDA. Mr. Moore—

MARC. Don't worry about me. I'm forming a new theory even as we speak.

LUCINDA *(turns back to TEDDY)*. Thank you, my love. *(LUCINDA heads off to the house. TEDDY watches after her.)*

MARC. Well, so long, Teddy. I wish you all the worst.

TEDDY. Could I trouble you for a cigarette? *(MARC looks up. He removes his gold box of cigarettes from his inside pocket.)*

MARC. Are you sure you can handle one of mine?

TEDDY. Certainly. In fact, I like them so much that I want the entire box.

MARC. You've recently acquired a great deal of nerve.

TEDDY. I don't mean for you to give them to me free of charge. I'm sure we could come to some kind of agreement. What if I drew up a contract? If you give me that box of cigarettes, I'll give you this castle.

MARC. I don't understand. *(TEDDY crouches near MARC and removes two sheaves of paper from his ledger.)*

TEDDY. Here's the deed. Look it over and see if you have any questions.

MARC. But I thought that that you'd sold it to the baron—

TEDDY. Oh, well, you see, I lied about that. You have to sign both copies.

MARC. Why are you doing this?

TEDDY *(shaking his head)*. I was so desperate for money today that I nearly signed this whole place over to the baron. And he'd plow up these gardens and make them as desolate as the rest of the countryside. How could I let that happen? This was all hers. I can't risk being that weak again. So I have to sell the castle to you.

MARC. But how do you know I won't turn right around and sell it to the baron?

TEDDY. Because: you've built a shack here that looks like a mansion and you've got a son here who looks like you. Plus you know as well as I do that if you'd managed to show Iris the slightest bit of affection, she'd still be alive. No, you'll never leave.

MARC. The truth is, I'm beginning to think that I'll never actually be able to leave any place. Or anyone, for that matter. And after all this... effort.

TEDDY. Sign before the pen goes dry. *(TEDDY gives the pen to MARC. MARC signs both copies of the deed. TEDDY takes back his copy. MARC hands him the box of cigarettes.)*

MARC. What will you say to your wife when you get back to the States and there's no money in the bank?

TEDDY. I'll lie to her. I'll tell her the baron's checks have been delayed. After what I've done today, I ought to be in her good graces for a long time. *(TEDDY lights a cigarette from MARC's box and takes a deep drag.)*

MARC. She said you were a wonderful businessman. She doesn't know the half of it, I'm afraid.

TEDDY. I'll put food in her mouth and clothes on her back. And that boy is the love of her life. I'll bring him up properly.. She's certainly not getting a raw deal.

MARC *(with a cry)*. You don't love her at all, do you? Why didn't you just let her go? If only to put her out of her misery.

TEDDY. You know why. *(MARC and TEDDY both stare off toward the house.)*

MARC. She *does* look almost exactly like Iris, doesn't she?

TEDDY. And you'd be amazed how much that can accomplish. *(TEDDY takes a last drag off the cigarette, tosses it to the ground, and extinguishes it with his foot. He holds out the box of cigarettes to MARC.)* I should go up to her. Would you like these?

MARC. Too strong for you after all?

TEDDY. No, I just can't afford the habit anymore.

MARC *(takes back the box of cigarettes)*. There's a lot you can't afford. I thought that a man in your position would have to surrender at least one or two of his illusions on a day like today. But somehow you've managed to maintain them all. And what's it cost you? Just several hundred thousand dollars.

TEDDY. Don't worry about me. I can promise you in a year I'll be a millionaire.

MARC *(with a sharp laugh)*. How can you be so sure?

TEDDY. I don't really know. But the past 11 years have been like crawling through mud for me. And then today—well, all of a sudden, it's like she's alive in the world again. Isn't that funny? *(Picking a flower on his way out.)* May I? It's for my wife.

MARC. Whatever you say. I wish you much happiness.

TEDDY. I wish you the same. Take care of all this for her, will you? *(TEDDY is gone. MARC stares after him. He retrieves his cane and braces himself with it. Slowly he stands, dusting himself off with his free hand, never taking his eyes from the house where TEDDY and LUCINDA are. Suddenly the heavens open. Rain pours down onto MARC's head. A sour smile forms on his lips. He turns his face to the sky.)*

MARC. Is that the best you can do?

END OF ACT TWO

ACT THREE

AT RISE: *A summer evening in 1947. The sun is low in the sky. There is a large hole in the roof of the gazebo. TEDDY and HOLLY stand just in front of it, conferring over an unwieldy paper map. TEDDY, in his early 20s, carries a small box under his arm. He is gentle, quiet, and nervous. HOLLY, in her late 20s, speaks with a light Texas accent. She is vivaciously mercurial, with a hidden melancholy streak.*

TEDDY. Are you sure this is it?

HOLLY. Absolutely not.

TEDDY. Then what good are you?

HOLLY. None at all. Lucky I'm the prettiest girl you've ever seen or you would've ditched me long ago. *(Pointing to the map.)* I think we came down this little red line here and then we turned on to this line. And this is the only castle for miles.

TEDDY *(peering up toward the castle)*. There don't seem to be any signs of life up there.

HOLLY. No, but there's a light in the window of that little house.

(A quick rustling of branches, and then MARC appears from deep in the garden. He is in his late 20s, dressed in dirty overalls, and carries a large, ancient rifle, which

he points directly at TEDDY. MARC is physically unkempt and verbally impeccable.)

MARC. *Qui est la?*

HOLLY. Dear God.

TEDDY *(to MARC, raising his arms). Je m'appelle*... Teddy. *(To HOLLY.)* Have you got the translation book?

HOLLY. I left it on the dashboard. *(MARC peers at them quizzically. When he speaks again, it is in faintly accented, fluent, although somewhat formal, English.)*

MARC. This is private property.

HOLLY. Oh, you speak American! I mean, you speak English. We're American.

TEDDY. We don't mean any harm, we're just...

MARC *(coming closer).* I'm being especially cautious tonight. It's the anniversary of the liberation of Belgium. Last year some boys from the village snuck out here and set off fireworks in the garden.

HOLLY *(showing the map to MARC).* I'm not going to humiliate myself by trying to pronounce these names. We want to be here. Are we?

MARC *(looking at the map, then, carefully, at HOLLY).* Yes. This is where you are.

HOLLY. I knew it! You don't mind if we take a look around, do you?

MARC. Indeed I do. You *are* trespassing, and it would be completely within the bounds of the law for me to shoot you in the head.

HOLLY. Now why be a spoilsport? Just a little stroll. *(Handing MARC some money.)* And there's no need to tell the master of the house.

MARC. First of all I'm not a servant and second of all these are drachma.

HOLLY *(taking the money back from MARC)*. What a dunce I am. We just came from Greece, and my daddy asked me to to bring him money from every country we visit.

TEDDY. This is your castle?

MARC. That's right.

TEDDY. But you're too young to be Marcus Moore.

MARC. I am Marcus Moore, Jr.

TEDDY. I'm Teddy Sterrett, Jr.

MARC. I remember your father. And I don't mean to be rude, but that only multiplies my desire to shoot you in the head.

TEDDY. And this is Holly.

HOLLY. You speak English awfully well.

MARC. My father taught me.

TEDDY. Would it be possible, do you think, for me to talk to your father?

MARC. He's dead.

TEDDY. I'm sorry. My father's passed on as well. A pair of orphans in the storm, I guess... Why I'm here: I should ask you, then. My father made an awfully strange last request. *(Taking a photograph from his pocket.)* He wanted me to burn this photograph with his ashes, and then he wanted his ashes scattered here in this garden.

MARC. You should've written me first about this.

TEDDY. I was afraid you'd say no.

MARC. Which is what I will say.

TEDDY. I do appeal to you, as a fellow orphan in the storm: I'd like to finally lay my father to rest. *(MARC takes the photograph from TEDDY and examines it closely. The photograph appears to have been ripped into tiny pieces and then carefully reassembled.)*

MARC. This is Iris Bell. There's a painting of her in the castle. *(To HOLLY.)* You look exactly like her.

HOLLY. Oh, you men, you think we're all the same woman. That's how I met Teddy. I was at a party in New York, and Teddy tapped me on the shoulder and said, "Excuse me, you look just like my mother." I thought, I haven't heard that one before.

TEDDY. So what do you say: will you help me?

MARC. That would be impossible.

TEDDY. Look, my father used to own this place—

MARC. And now I own it.

TEDDY. —and this was the last thing he asked me to do. I've been waiting three years. We came God knows how many thousand miles. If you'd just leave us alone for five minutes, we'll do this and then we'll go and you'll never even know we were here.

MARC. No.

TEDDY. Why not?

MARC. I don't have to explain myself to you.

TEDDY. Could I at least take a walk around? It would mean a great deal to me, more than you could possibly know, if I could just see the place.

MARC. If it means that much to you, absolutely not.

HOLLY *(digging around in her purse)*. I'm sure I've got some actual francs in here. *(Triumphantly pulling out some bills.)* Here you go: 2000. That's my final offer.

TEDDY. You don't have to—

MARC. You'd pay 2000 francs for a walk in the garden? Are you stupid?

HOLLY. I guess so. What do you say? *(HOLLY holds the bills out to MARC. MARC considers and then, smiling a little, takes the bills out of her hand.)*

MARC. Leave the box here.

TEDDY *(puts the box down and turns to HOLLY)*. Do you want to come along?

HOLLY. I think I'll rest my weary bones, if you don't mind. But hold on a minute, buster. Am I the prettiest girl you've ever seen?

TEDDY. You just said you were.

HOLLY. I know, but you can't take my word for anything.

TEDDY *(considers for a moment, then:)*. Prettiest girl I've ever seen.

HOLLY. Hurry back. *(TEDDY disappears further into the garden. HOLLY looks after him, letting some of her good spirits burn away into exhaustion. She pulls out a whiskey flask.)* Hey, you. Yeah, you, Prince of Darkness. You want a belt?

MARC. No, thank you.

HOLLY. Don't mind if I do myself. *(Takes a stiff belt and sits down in the gazebo.)* I love what you've done here. Most people would put a solid roof on top of the gazebo, but this is so much more striking.

MARC. Oh, that. A tree fell on it a few years ago and I haven't had time to fix it.

HOLLY. Yeah, I guess things must get pretty hectic around here. *(Pause.)* Do you think you could find it in your heart to help Teddy? He wants this more than anything.

MARC. I suppose he must have loved his father very much.

HOLLY. Cancer took his momma when he was 16. He doesn't have any family left in the world.

MARC. It will do no good to play on my sympathy.

HOLLY. If you want money, my daddy's rich.

MARC. It's not the money.

HOLLY. What *is* it, then? Honor? Or are you just a heartless son of a bitch?

MARC *(smiling slightly)*. I *do* have a hole in my heart. It gives me an extra heartbeat. It goes boom, boom, shh.

HOLLY. I don't believe you.

MARC. Put your hand right here and you can feel it.

HOLLY. This is just one of those tricks you've got worked up to get the girls to touch you. *(But HOLLY comes closer to MARC and puts her hand carefully on his heart.)* Well, I'll be damned.

MARC. When I was a boy, my father told me I was born with my heart already broken. He said that would save a pretty girl the trouble of breaking it for me.

HOLLY *(taking her hand away from MARC's heart)*. Your daddy wasn't much of a romantic.

MARC. My father thought everything was extremely significant. He couldn't blow out a candle without making it a metaphor for the decline and fall of mankind.

HOLLY. My daddy doesn't think anything's significant. No regrets, he always says.

MARC. Why should he have any regrets? He's rich.

HOLLY. He was dirt poor most of his life, following the booms and working on the rigs. Every once in a while he'd save up enough money to buy some land to drill for himself. I'll say one thing for my daddy, he could take a failure better than anybody I've ever met. He must've drilled and come up dry 20 times, still he'd manage to get up the next morning pretty much whole. Then just after my momma died he bought this patch of dirt in

Desdemona that nobody wanted because it'd been salted a thousand feet deep. He stuck a testing tool in there, and all the trees downwind were drenched with oil. And we were rich.

MARC. Just like that?

HOLLY. Just like that...I'm gonna stand a little further away from you because otherwise you'll fall hopelessly in love with me.

MARC. What makes you think I'm going to fall in love with you?

HOLLY. I'm the prettiest girl you've ever seen. You already have a huge crush on me. You brought me flowers.

MARC. What flowers?

HOLLY. This whole garden.

MARC. This garden was planted by an old American woman who left it to her daughter, who left it to Teddy's father, who sold it to my father, who left it to me. And all this before any of us had ever laid eyes on you.

HOLLY. Well, do you know what I think? They were all in love with me, all those people, they just didn't know it because they'd never met me. And without even knowing why, they tended these flowers for 50 years, just so I could come along today and look at them. Whose job is it to take care of this garden, anyway?

MARC. It's mine.

HOLLY. Well, if you don't mind my saying so, you've let the place go to pieces.

MARC. That's right. When it rains I let the ditches fill with water till the soil's too drenched to grow anything new. When it doesn't rain I keep the ground parched. And I let the weeds choke whatever flowers arc still lcft. And on the first of every month a few francs are delivered to my door regardless. It's a wonderful arrangement. It's my revenge.

HOLLY. Revenge? On who?

MARC. On everyone.

HOLLY. Well, you've really pulled one over on us, haven't you? *(Pause.)* Your daddy left America for this? Why on earth?

MARC. I don't know. I've never been anywhere but here.

HOLLY. Well, we have to take you to America. You're practically a citizen.

MARC. I don't have any money.

HOLLY. Consider it a swap. You let Teddy do what he wants tonight, and I'll buy this castle from you and pay your way to America.

MARC. I didn't know that we'd started discussing business again.

HOLLY. Oh, handsome, we never stopped discussing business. I'm friendly but I'm not that friendly. And if you really don't care about this place, why not help Teddy out?

MARC. Why is it so important to you?

HOLLY. Because he asked me to marry him on the boat over.

MARC. I suppose congratulations are in order.

HOLLY. I haven't said yes yet.

MARC. In my opinion you should accept his offer as soon as possible. You'll no longer have anything to offer when you no longer have your beauty.

HOLLY *(deeply stung)*. That's what money's for, isn't it?

MARC. I wouldn't know.

HOLLY. I would. When I was a girl I was kicked out of more drugstores and cafes than I would care to count. And now I can walk in any place like the queen of England. Contrary to popular belief, money *can* buy you happiness. It can also buy you love. And it can certainly buy *you*. So tell me: how much will it take to get you to help Teddy? I'm willing to pay.

MARC. Thank you, but I am afraid you are not in possession of the proper currency.

HOLLY. Well, that's too bad. Here I thought we could help each other out. Something awful must've happened to you, handsome. Whatever it was, I'm sorry.

(TEDDY comes back in from the garden carrying some wildflowers, which he presents to HOLLY.)

TEDDY. Flowers for the prettiest girl I've ever seen.

HOLLY. I tried to bargain with this boy, Teddy. I even offered to take him to America, but he won't budge.

MARC. In fact, I think we might be able to come to a bargain. If I could speak with him alone.

HOLLY *(smiling, surprised)*. By all means. I've got a bottle of champagne in the car with your name on it. Do nothing till you hear from me. *(HOLLY gives TEDDY a light kiss and strolls out of the garden. TEDDY and MARC consider each other.)*

MARC. Do you want some bread? It's gone stale so I'm not going to eat it. *(MARC takes some bread out of his pocket and tosses it to TEDDY. MARC picks up the rifle and sits on the gazebo railing, aiming out into the garden.)*

TEDDY. Thank you... what are you doing?

MARC. Shooting pigeons. They're dirty, filthy little birds, they do nothing but shit on the flowers. I'm sick of taking care of the place but I must confess I'm still quite fond of this particular duty. *(MARC gives a little shout, then quickly aims his rifle and pulls the trigger. He surveys his handiwork, grinning with pleasure.)*

TEDDY. I guess the war must have been very hard on you.

MARC. The funny thing about Belgium is that it was supposed to be neutral during the war. England and France and Germany all got together and designated it, what is the term, a no-man's land. A principality all its own. Of course, as soon as the war begins, they find this arrangement deeply inconvenient. And the first thing they do is charge through this principality, destroying villages and forests and people who only ask and expect to be left alone.

TEDDY. You lost your father in the war, didn't you?

MARC. It was very dangerous for Americans to be here during the occupation. I'm sure you know that.

TEDDY. I'm very sorry.

MARC. It isn't your fault.

TEDDY. I fought over here, with the 11th Armored.

MARC. The 11th Armored. I met one or two of the 11th Armored. What did you call yourselves? The Flashes of Lightning?

TEDDY. The Thunderbolts.

MARC. The Thunderbolts, yes. What an unruly bunch of boys.

TEDDY. It was the first time I'd ever seen Europe. Of course most of what I saw had already been bombed to smithereens. Here in Belgium, and then in Luxembourg, which was the stupidest place in the world to fight.

Trudging through mud and snow for days on end to take back mountains that nobody in his right mind would ever want. I heard Austria was beautiful, but I was sent home before I had the chance to see it.

MARC. When you were sent home, it was not because you were injured, was it? Did you have a ... a collapse?

TEDDY. I was sick for a while ... you said you were willing to bargain?

MARC. I certainly did. I will let you scatter your father's ashes here, if you will answer for me one question and grant for me one request.

TEDDY. I guess that depends on the question and the request.

MARC. These are my terms. If you fulfill them, I promise to let you do what you want. If not, you must go home and never return. So?

TEDDY. I don't have any choice.

MARC. Tell me how you went mad.

TEDDY. I beg your pardon.

MARC. My question is, what was it like for you to go mad? Did you see things? Did it happen all at once or little by little? And how did you regain your mind? What was it all like for you?

TEDDY. You wouldn't be willing to ask me another question?

MARC. If you don't wish to answer, I understand. But then you forfeit the terms of our bargain.

TEDDY *(considers for a long moment, then:)*. I remember carrying a wounded man on my shoulders, and then I remember the sound of airplanes strafing us overhead. And then I remember what seemed like a hailstorm at my back, and I felt the life drain out of the guy on my shoulders. And then I remember throwing him to the ground and starting to cry. I didn't feel crazy. The truth is, I felt it was a pretty rational response under the circumstances.

MARC. I suppose it probably was.

TEDDY. In the hospital I felt like I was going crazy. There was a real pull toward that, you know, you see all these soldier boys with dead eyes, humming old high school fight songs 24 hours a day, you think, that's not such a bad way to be.

MARC. This morning I woke up and I thought, please, let today be the day I finally go mad. I've been absolutely alone here for four years, I've lost both my parents, I've seen my countryside destroyed. I see this garden, I stopped tending it but it won't die. It ought to be too much for me by now. I am quite sickened, to be honest, by my capacity to endure all this. *(MARC gives another shout, and fires the rifle. He smiles triumphantly. He turns and holds the rifle out to TEDDY.)* Would you like to try? *(TEDDY considers for a moment, and then takes the rifle from MARC. He aims out into the garden and fires.)*

TEDDY. Damn!

MARC. You can't shoot them when they're in the air. You have to wait until they land and then you flush them out. Tell me when you see another one and I'll show you.

TEDDY. And now? Your request?

MARC. My request, yes. Give me whatever is in your pockets. Except for your money: this is not a robbery.

TEDDY. I don't understand.

MARC. It would be a tremendous sacrifice for me to allow you to scatter your father's ashes here. If I am to permit this I need to know that you will be making a comparable sacrifice. So. May I take whatever you have in your pockets? *(TEDDY considers for a moment. He digs in his pockets. He removes some change and a small black case. MARC passes over the change and opens the case.)* These are your medals from the war?

TEDDY. That's right.

MARC. You must've been very brave.

TEDDY. I guess. *(MARC continues searching through TEDDY's pockets, as yet, coming up empty-handed.)*

MARC. You travel very lightly. I am impressed. *(Removing a letter from TEDDY's pocket.)* What's this?

TEDDY. It's a letter from my father. I got it when I was over here, just a few days after he died.

MARC. Your father died young as well, then.

TEDDY. Forty-five years old and the richest man in New York.

MARC *(holding the letter up)*. May I?

TEDDY. It's yours now, isn't it?

MARC *(opening the letter and reading)*. "Dear Teddy: I am very surprised that you were one of the men responsible for the capture of Neufchateau-Bastogne. I never thought of you as a particularly brave boy. I must attribute your success to the inadequacy of the German Army. You should know that I have a very special feeling for Belgium. A woman named Iris Bell once gave me a castle there as a present." *(Looking up from the letter.)* Iris Bell must've been a very special woman.

TEDDY. It gets even better.

MARC. "I've enclosed a photograph of her. You may think at first glance that she looks like your mother. I take great pains to assure you that your mother was only a pale replica of Iris. I say all this because the hour is late for me. After I've died I shall be burnt, and I want you to take my ashes, burn this photograph in with them, and scatter them in Iris's garden. I believe that you owe me this tribute. Your father, Theodore." *(Putting the letter in his pocket.)* I hope that he left you a great deal of money.

TEDDY. None at all. When I was a boy he said if there was any money coming to me I'd turn soft, and that's the worst thing in the world to be.

MARC. So where is the money?

TEDDY. His entire fortune was willed to the care and maintenance of these gardens.

MARC. May I ask, if your father was such a cruel man, why have you come all the way here at his command?

TEDDY. I don't know.

MARC. When I was a boy I idolized King Albert. Everybody did, but I did especially, because I was only half-Belgian and I felt a great need to compensate. Then one day—I guess I was 13 or 14—King Albert went climbing in the Ardennes and he fell off a mountain and died. Which should have been a lesson to me in the fallibility of kings.

TEDDY. That's funny. I'd take that as a lesson in the dangers of mountain-climbing. *(It takes a moment for MARC to get the joke, but once he does he roars with laughter. TEDDY can't help but join in. At the top of MARC's laugh:)*

MARC. I don't think I could hate any place worse than this. It stinks of the Germans and the mines and my father's anger. And what's worse is I'm starting to stink of all those things myself. I'd leave in a second if I could only figure out some place I could call home.

TEDDY. You sound like an American to me. Through and through. *(Peering out into the garden.)* I see one.

MARC. All right. Now aim. A little higher. I'll count to three, and then I'll flush him out, and then you shoot. All right. One, two, three ... *(MARC lets out a sharp yell. TEDDY fires. They both stare out.)* Perfect. *(Pause.)* Do you know, my friend, I think you're welcome to do whatever you want here. I just don't want to see. *(MARC reaches into his pockets and gives the medals and the letter back to TEDDY.)*

TEDDY. Thank you. *(But MARC is already gone. TEDDY sits alone in the gazebo.)*

(HOLLY comes into the garden. She carries a wicker basket that contains a bottle of champagne and two glasses.)

HOLLY. Did you miss me?

TEDDY. I was about to send out a search party.

HOLLY. I was skulking around the castle.

TEDDY. I've been given permission to bury my father here.

HOLLY. How wonderful! That's everything you wanted, isn't it?

TEDDY. Almost everything. *(TEDDY's statement hangs in the air. The two of them consider each other delicately.)*

HOLLY. You know, when I was a girl I played Knights of the Round Table with Eddie Wink during sandstorms. He was Lancelot and I was Guinevere caught by the evil dust dragon. This doesn't look anything like the castles in my imagination.

TEDDY. No. It isn't anything like I imagined either.

HOLLY. Still. It'd be nice to own a castle.

TEDDY. When my father looked at this place, what did he see? *(The sound of fireworks. Faint colored shadows illuminate their faces.)*

HOLLY. Oh, I love fireworks! What are they for?

TEDDY. It's the anniversary of victory and peace.

HOLLY. Isn't that sweet.

TEDDY. Once in a town near here I found a little kid nearly starved to death. I picked him up and carried him back to camp.

HOLLY. What a hero you were.

TEDDY. No. Nothing like that.

HOLLY. It was good of you to come all the way over here. I'm sure your daddy's grateful, wherever he is.

TEDDY. The truth is, I didn't come because he asked me to. I came because I wanted to understand. But I don't.

HOLLY. Do you know who I look the most like? *My* momma. She starved herself to give me square meals, and she died less than a month before life got easy for us. That sorrow is the principal thing I own. And I can't get rid of it. If I run away it catches up to me. If I bury it in the ground it takes root and grows. All I can do is wrap my arms around a handsome boy and look at all the victory and peace lighting up the sky. And so close! I bet if I stood on your shoulders I could touch it.

TEDDY. Goddamnit, Holly, you're the prettiest girl I've ever seen.

HOLLY *(very quietly and simply)*. Am I? Really?

TEDDY *(tenderly)*. I don't think I could kiss another girl without thinking of you. You've ruined me forever.

HOLLY. Have I?

TEDDY. Yes, thank you. *(HOLLY considers him very closely. For a long moment, just the sound of fireworks.)*

HOLLY. Oh, please, please, marry me. Marry me right this instant. *(HOLLY and TEDDY stare at each other for a long moment. TEDDY leans in and kisses her on the mouth. She responds.)*

(MARC pokes his head back into the garden.)

MARC. Excuse me, but...have you finished already?

TEDDY. No, I...haven't even begun. *(To HOLLY.)* I guess there's no point in waiting any longer.

HOLLY. I guess not.

(HOLLY picks up the box. TEDDY removes the photograph from his pocket. MARC takes out his gold box of cigarettes. He opens the box and takes out a match. He strikes the match against the side of the gazebo and lights the bottom of the photograph. TEDDY lets the burnt photograph fall into the box. HOLLY hands the box to TEDDY. TEDDY moves into the garden. He takes ashes from the box and lets them fall through his fingers. The dusk light casts shadows of blue and gold against the ashes as they scatter to the winds and the ground. HOLLY and MARC watch intently. TEDDY finishes and comes down to HOLLY. HOLLY embraces him)

HOLLY *(taking a deep breath)*. Now: champagne! *(To MARC.)* Would you do the honors? There're only two glasses but I'm happy to drink from the bottle. *(MARC takes the bottle from HOLLY and uncorks it with a loud pop. HOLLY pours TEDDY and MARC glasses of champagne and raises the bottle in the air.)* A toast. Teddy and Marc: here's to your fathers. I never met them, so I don't know what they were really like, but it's a safe bet that they weren't how you remember them. They *were* responsible for the two of you, so they couldn't have been all bad.

MARC. Very good.

TEDDY. Hear hear. *(MARC and TEDDY clink their glasses against HOLLY's bottle. They down their drinks.)*

MARC. Would you mind very much if I made a toast as well?

HOLLY. Of course not. *(HOLLY refills their glasses.)*

MARC. I'd like to offer this to the two of you. This has been without a doubt the most absurd night of my life. And if you are still willing to bargain with me, I want very much to sell this castle to you.

HOLLY. Do you mean it?

MARC. Just pay me enough money so I can get out of here forever.

HOLLY. I think I can manage that. *(Night is beginning to overtake the garden. In the dusk, the figures inside the gazebo start to become less distinct, more hazy. To TEDDY.)* I think you have a toast to make.

TEDDY *(considers for a moment, then:)*. To everything I wanted. *(They all touch glasses and drink. It's getting harder to see them clearly.)*

HOLLY. What are we all doing so far from home?

MARC. How soon can we leave?

TEDDY. How soon can you get packed?

MARC. I'm taking nothing with me.

HOLLY. Wait! I'm the new princess of this castle, and nobody's going anywhere until I get a dance. Come on, let's cut up a rug. *(HOLLY extends her arm to MARC. MARC considers, and then tentatively and awkwardly starts to dance with her, then:)*

MARC. I think I'll sit this one out. *(MARC steps aside. TEDDY moves in and dances with HOLLY. He kisses her and spins her around, pulling away so he can get a better look at her.)*

TEDDY. More! More! More... *(HOLLY stands quietly, considering her surroundings as if for the first time.)*

HOLLY. You brought me all these flowers. *(The last ray of sunlight flickers across their faces, and then surrenders itself to the horizon. The garden and the revelers are lost to the night.)*

END OF PLAY

DIRECTOR'S NOTES

DIRECTOR'S NOTES